MAGIC TRICKS

COIN MAGIC

Written by
JOHN WOOD

Gareth Stevens
PUBLISHING

Please visit our website, www.garethstevens.com.
For a free color catalog of all our high-quality books,
call toll free 1-800-542-2595 or fax 1-877-542-2596.

Cataloging-in-Publication Data

Names: Wood, John.
Title: Coin magic / John Wood.
Description: New York : Gareth Stevens Publishing, 2019. | Series: Magic tricks | Includes glossary and index.
Identifiers: LCCN ISBN 9781538226032 (pbk.) | ISBN 9781538226025 (library bound) |
ISBN 9781538226049 (6 pack)
Subjects: LCSH: Coin tricks--Juvenile literature .
Classification: LCC GV1559W663 2019 | DDC 793.8--dc23

First Edition

Published in 2019 by
Gareth Stevens Publishing
111 East 14th Street, Suite 349
New York, NY 10003

© 2018 Booklife Publishing
This edition is published in arrangement with Booklife Publishing

Produced for Gareth Stevens by Booklife
Editor: Kirsty Holmes
Designer: Danielle Jones

Picture credits: Cover & 1 – Pretty Vectors. 2 – LiliGraphie, Oksana Shufrych, Kat_Branch, Katja
Gerasimova, chelovector. 3 – fox18002, Macrovector. 4 – AngeloDeVal, Mantana Boonsatr. 5 – Watercolor_
swallow. 6 – jocic, Michael C. Gray. 7 – Elnur. 8 – George Starke [Public domain], via Wikimedia
Commons, rzstudio. 9 – sagir, Andrey Lobachev. 10 – Premium Photography, Jay Crihfield, nvaluwan,
Dmitri Ma. 11 – By GooDween123, jannoon028. 12 – exopixel. 13 – Ruslan Ivantsov, artproem. 14 –
1JMueller, Thomas Nelson Downs (The Art of Magic. The Downs-Edwards Company, 1909.) [Public
domain], via Wikimedia Commons. 15 – GOLFX, Feng Yu. 16 – Victoruler, koosen, Olena Chilikina.
17 – Alfa Photostudio, photolinc, PachetoKZ. 18 – Danny Smythe, Studio DMM Photography, Designs &
Art. 19 – Boonyarit Sribal, Mega Pixel, PowerUp. 20 – Claudio Divizia, Fat Jackey. 21 – Champion studio.
22 – Nagy-Bagoly Arpad. 23 – Fat Jackey, Picsfive. 24 – Michael C. Gray, Africa Studio, Syda P , stockce.
25 – Phongphan. 26 – xmee, By juhanaaa. 27 – Komkrit Noenpoempisut, atipp, Andrey_Kuzmin. 28 –
haveseen. 29 – Evgeny Karandaev,, Savelov Maksim, Syda Productions, Oleksii Biriukov. 30 – Neungstockr.
Images are courtesy of Shutterstock.com. With thanks to Getty Images, Thinkstock Photo and iStockphoto.

Printed in the United States of America

CPSIA compliance information: Batch #CS18GS:
For further information contact Gareth Stevens, New York, New York at 1-800-542-2595.

COIN MAGIC
CONTENTS

Words that look like **this** are explained in the glossary on page 31.

CAN YOU KEEP A SECRET?

So, you want to be a magician? Well, you've come to the right place. There are many secrets waiting for you inside this book. By the time you're finished reading, you will be a master of coin magic. Let's begin!

COINS

In many of these tricks you will need to hide coins in your hands. Coins come in all shapes and sizes, and it is important to find the right kind of coin for you. If, for example, you have small hands, you might want to use smaller coins.

DID YOU KNOW?

Coins are popular in magic because they are easy to hide – with enough practice!

THE HISTORY OF COIN MAGIC

Coin magic has been <u>performed</u> for hundreds and hundreds of years. One of the earliest books that mentions coin magic is called *The Discoverie of Witchcraft*. It was written in 1584. Back then, magic was thought to be done by scary witches and mysterious fortune tellers.

COIN MAGIC TODAY

Nowadays, coin magic is performed by magicians and entertainers at birthday parties and at magic shows. Usually, coin magic is performed to smaller groups of people because coins are small and people need to be close up.

A witch was a woman who practiced evil magic.

Coin magic is performed all over the world, in all sorts of places.

DID YOU KNOW?

A group of witches was called a coven. They were said to perform an evil type of magic called <u>black magic</u>.

MAGIC LESSON: SLEIGHT OF HAND

If you want to do coin magic, you have to be good with your hands. There is a special term for quick, clever hand movements: it is called sleight of hand. Magicians use sleight of hand to make objects disappear, **reappear** or switch places.

ANGLES

When doing sleight of hand, you need to think about what the audience can see. The angle between their eyes and your hands is important – are they looking down onto your hands? Are they farther away, or sitting down? When you are hiding coins in your hand, you need to make sure you are not accidentally showing the audience.

Practicing in front of a mirror is helpful. It will help you see what your audience will see.

SLEIGHT OF HAND

takes a lot of practice. Before you perform a sleight of hand trick for an audience, practice it over and over again until it looks quick and natural.

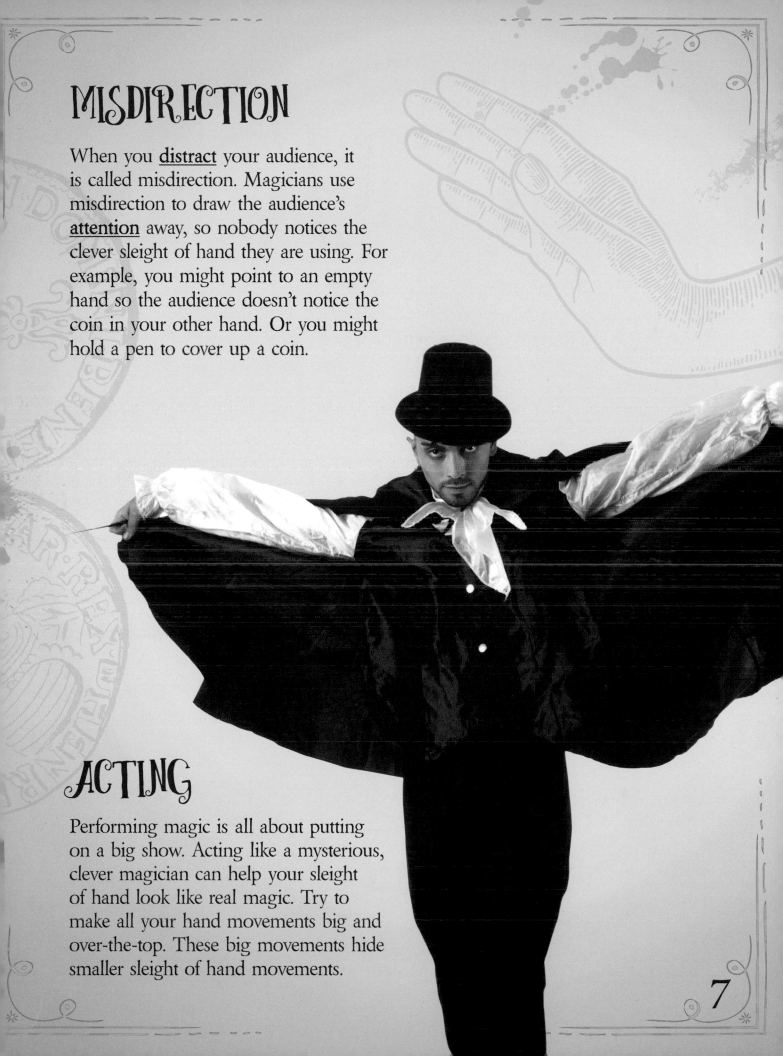

MISDIRECTION

When you <u>distract</u> your audience, it is called misdirection. Magicians use misdirection to draw the audience's <u>attention</u> away, so nobody notices the clever sleight of hand they are using. For example, you might point to an empty hand so the audience doesn't notice the coin in your other hand. Or you might hold a pen to cover up a coin.

ACTING

Performing magic is all about putting on a big show. Acting like a mysterious, clever magician can help your sleight of hand look like real magic. Try to make all your hand movements big and over-the-top. These big movements hide smaller sleight of hand movements.

7

COIN THROUGH A TABLE TRICK

For your first trick, you will make a coin go through a solid table. There are no special coins or tables involved, just sleight of hand and a bit of acting. This will leave your audience amazed!

This trick was invented by a famous magician named Tony Slydini, who was very good at close-up magic. Slydini toured the world, performing his magic tricks with clever sleight of hand. This trick is a really good place to start learning coin magic.

THERE IS

no **preparation** for this trick, which means you can perform it whenever somebody asks.

Tony Slydini

YOU WILL NEED...

⫷ Coin

⫷ Table

THIS TRICK works best when the audience is on the other side of the table, but can't see underneath.

STEP 1

Put a coin on a table. Point to it and tell the audience that you are going to make it go through the table.

DURING

the first three steps, keep one hand on your lap, <u>palm</u> up, so you are ready to catch the coin when you slide it off the table.

STEP 2

Slide the coin to the edge of the table, near your <u>lap</u>.

STEP 3

In one movement, slide the coin off the table while pretending to pick it up. Pretend to hold the coin between your thumb and fingers, but keep your palm facing your chest, so the audience can't actually see what is in your hand.

STEP 4

Pretend to tap the coin three times on the table. At the same time, use your other hand to actually tap the coin on the underside of the table.

STEP 5

Now slam your hand onto the table so your palm is flat. At the same time, hit the underneath of the table with the coin.

STEP 6

Flip your hand on top of the table to show that there is no coin. Now bring your other hand from underneath the table and show the coin. Tell the audience that it went through the table!

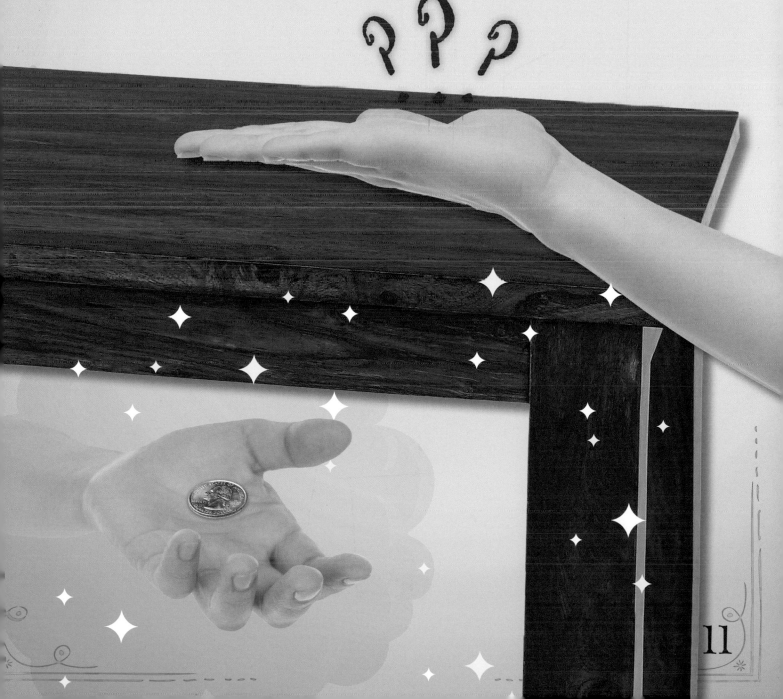

MAGIC LESSON:
PALMING A COIN

When a magician hides a coin in their hand, it is called palming a coin. Palming coins is one of the most important parts of coin magic. If the audience doesn't know exactly where a coin really is, you can make them think the coin is disappearing or reappearing. We are going to learn two types of coin palms.

FINGER PALM

In a finger palm, the coin rests near the ring finger, between the point where the finger and hand meet and the middle **knuckle**. If you curl your middle, ring and little fingers a tiny bit, the coin won't fall out, no matter how much you move your hand. Make sure you keep your fingers close enough together that the audience won't see the coin through any gaps. Keep your palm facing down or away from the audience to hide the coin.

Many objects can be palmed, including cards.

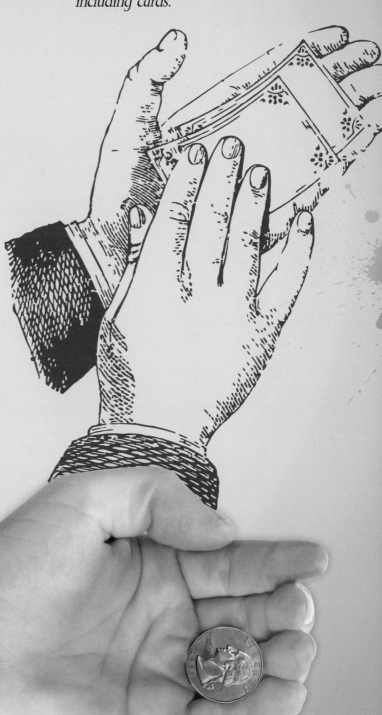

CLASSIC PALM

In the classic palm, the coin is placed directly in the middle of the palm. It is held in place by the hand muscles near the thumb. Bring your thumb closer to your palm so the coin stays locked in place. When using this palm, keep your other fingers loose and outstretched to make it look like your hand is empty.

Try to keep the hand as relaxed as you can. Hands and fingers are **naturally** curled, and you can use this to grip a palmed coin. Look at how a hand looks when it is empty and try to get yours to look like that as much as you can, even when you've palmed a coin.

From above, your hand should look normal and relaxed.

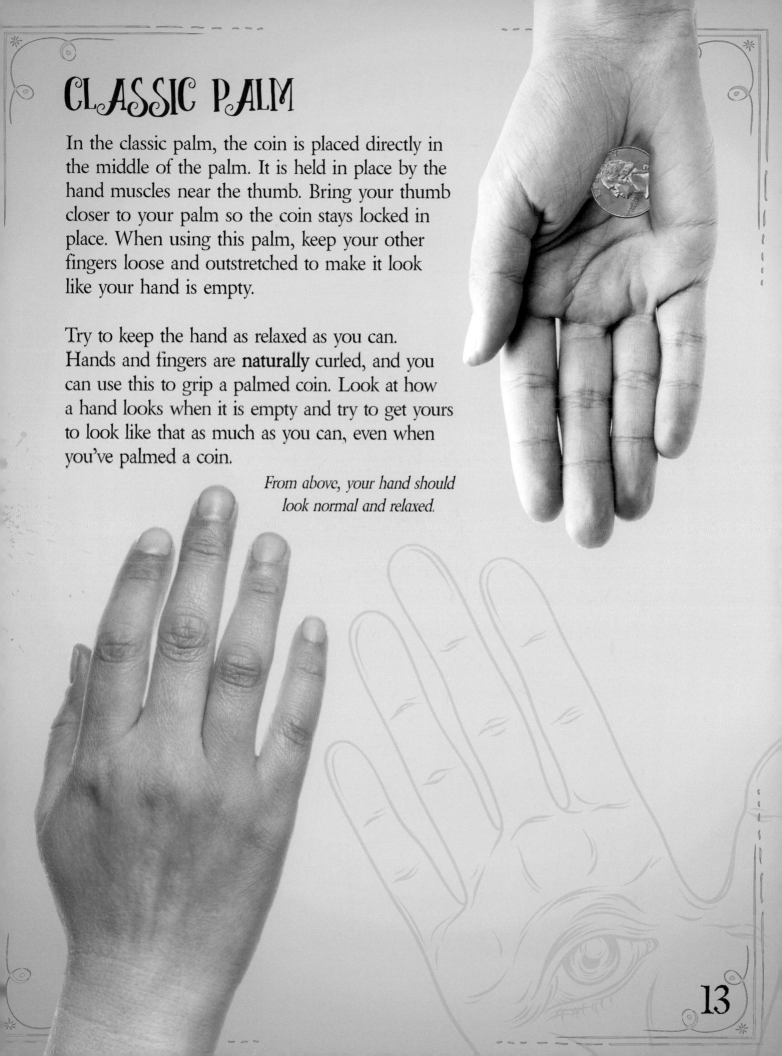

COIN THROUGH A CUP
TRICK

Our next trick is also about passing a coin through an object. By palming coins, you are going to make your audience think you have magically put a coin into a cup from underneath!

Thomas Nelson Downs was one of the most famous magicians to use coins in his magic tricks. His nickname was the "King of Koins." He performed magic around the world in the late 1800s, especially in England and Europe.

Cups are used in lots of magic tricks.

Thomas Nelson Downs

DID YOU KNOW?

Thomas Nelson Downs could apparently palm up to 60 coins at once.

YOU WILL NEED...

A cup that you can't see through

Two coins that look the same

Table

STEP 1

Using the classic palm, palm a coin in your left hand.

MAKE SURE

you do step 1 in **private**.

STEP 2

Put the second coin on the table, next to the cup. Show the audience that your cup is empty.

STEP 3

Using the left hand with the palmed coin, hold the cup from the top. Your palm should be positioned over the cup.

STEP 4

Put the second coin in your right hand palm, so the audience can see. Explain that you are going to push the coin through the bottom of the cup.

X2

STEP 5

Hit your open palm against the bottom of the cup twice.

STEP 6

The third time you do this, keep your right palm wedged against the bottom of the cup. At the same time, drop the coin from your left hand into the cup.

STEP 7

While holding the cup from the bottom in your right hand, tip the cup so the coin falls out. Watch as your audience is amazed!

17

CIRCLE COIN
PREDICTION TRICK

Throughout history, many people have said that they could **predict** the future. These people were called fortune-tellers. Fortune-tellers used crystal balls, tea leaves, and **tarot cards** to tell someone what was in store for them.

Nostradamus was a doctor who wrote down many predictions of the future. Some people think that he predicted lots of events such as the Great Fire of London, the death of a king named Henry II, and World War II. Other people think his predictions were **vague** and didn't mean anything.

Crystal Ball

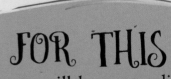

FOR THIS

trick you will be pretending to predict which coin the audience will choose. But there'll be no crystal balls or tea leaves – just six coins, each with a different shape.

Nostradamus

YOU WILL NEED...

Envelope

Six coins that look the same

Permanent marker

Table

Piece of paper

STEP 1

Before the trick, write on the piece of paper "In the end, you will be left with the circle."

STEP 2

Put the paper in the envelope. Now lay the coins out in a row on the table and draw a circle on the left-most coin. Now flip it over so it looks blank.

In the end, you will be left with the circle.

STEP 3

Call your audience in. Explain that you are going to perform a magic trick where you predict the future. Ask them to give you six simple shapes. As they say a shape, draw that shape on a coin. Make sure you don't draw any other shapes on the left-most coin. When they say circle, draw another circle on the left-most coin.

STEP 4

Ask an audience member to put a hand out flat, palm facing upwards. Take the coins and put them in the audience member's hand.

MAKE SURE the circle coin doesn't accidentally flip over at any point.

STEP 5

Ask them to put their other hand on top of the coins and shake the coins around.

STEP 6

Now open their hands to show the coins. Any coins that are face-down without a shape on them should be put on the table.

STEP 7

Keep asking them to shake the coins until there is only one coin left. Because the circle coin has shapes on both sides, the last coin will always be the circle!

STEP 8

Once they are left with the circle, put the coin on the table and take your piece of paper from the envelope. You can now <u>reveal</u> that you predicted the circle all along!

In the end, you will be left with the circle.

THE DISAPPEARING COIN TRICK

This time we are going to make a coin disappear by using a piece of paper and a trusty magic wand. The magic wand is just a **prop**, of course – you are the one who is doing all the magic!

Props are often used by magicians for misdirection. If the audience thinks that the wand is important, they will be distracted from the sleight of hand.

When using a magic wand, magicians might wave it around and say a magic word.

Magician's Props

YOU WILL NEED...

Coin

Piece of paper

THE PIECE
of paper shouldn't be too big.
It should be about the size
of a playing card.

Put your wand in your pocket
before the trick starts. You'll
need it later!

Magic
wand

STEP 1

Hold the coin up between your thumb and finger, and cover it with the paper, so it is hidden from the audience.

STEP 2

Fold the top of the paper backwards over the coin towards you. Only cover half of the coin.

EACH OF
the folds in step 3 should be made in the direction away from you. If you do this, there should be a gap at the bottom of the paper that the audience can't see.

STEP 3

Fold the left side over towards the audience, so it covers the side of the coin that is facing the audience. Do the same with the right side of the paper and the bottom of the paper.

STEP 4

Hold the paper-covered coin in your hand, between your thumb and fingers. Your palm should be positioned underneath, facing upwards. Keep your fingers together, so there are no gaps to see through.

STEP 5

Explain that you are going to make the coin disappear. As you are talking, let the coin slip out of the gap at the bottom, into your hand. Keep this coin palmed and hidden.

STEP 6

Switch the paper into your left hand and say that you need to get your magic wand from your pocket. With your right hand, drop the coin into your pocket and grab the wand.

STEP 7

Tap the paper with the wand. You could also say some magic words. Now you can open up the paper to reveal that the coin has disappeared!

MAGIC LESSON:
TRANSFERS

Sometimes you need to pretend to put a coin in one hand, but keep it in another. This is called a transfer. When doing a transfer, it is important to act like the coin has really changed hands. Let's learn two different transfers.

FRENCH DROP

STEP 1

Hold a coin in one hand between your thumb and fingers. Your palm should be facing up. Hold the coin by the edges so the audience can clearly see it.

STEP 2

Bring your other hand over the coin, palm down, and slide your thumb under the coin.

STEP 3

As you close this top hand and pretend to grab it, secretly drop the coin into your palm facing up.

STEP 4

Clench your top hand in a fist, as if the coin is inside. In the other hand, finger palm the coin. You can **casually** put this hand by your side. The audience won't know that the top hand is actually empty.

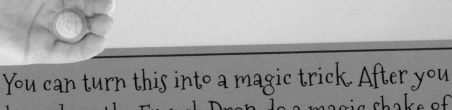

You can turn this into a magic trick. After you have done the French Drop, do a magic shake of your clenched, empty hand and pretend to make the coin disappear!

SHUTTLE PASS TRANSFER

For this transfer, you will need two coins that look the same. You will need a palmed coin in each hand.

STEP 1
Show the audience a coin in one of your hands.

STEP 2
Act as if you are tossing it into the other hand.

STEP 3
However, all you are doing is turning one palm up as the other one flips over.

STEP 4
If you time it right, it looks like you've tossed the coin over to the other hand.

STEP 5
Now you can pretend to put this second coin in your pocket, and mysteriously produce another coin from the first hand! Of course, the coins just stay in your hands the whole time.

After you've practiced these transfers enough, you can perform these as magic tricks in front of an audience.

TWO IN THE HAND

The last trick in this book is especially clever. Using some sleight of hand, you are going to make coins **teleport** from your pocket to your hand. At the end of the trick, they will all disappear!

YOU WILL NEED...

Four coins that look exactly the same

Table

DURING THIS trick, keep talking to the audience. Tell them what you want them to believe, such as "two coins are going into this hand," or "one coin is going into my pocket".

STEP 1

Palm a coin in your left hand.
Do this in private.

STEP 2

Put the other 3 coins in a row on the table, in front of the audience. Tell them you are going to make coins teleport from your pocket to your hands. Put two of the coins in your left hand.

STEP 3

Now pretend to put the last coin from the table in your pocket, but really finger palm the coin and keep it in your right hand.

STEP 4

Ask your audience how many coins are in your left hand. They should say two. Do a magic shake with your left hand. Now drop the 3 coins on the table.

STEP 5

Tell the audience you'll show them again. Put two of the coins on the table into your right hand. Put the last coin from the table in your pocket.

STEP 6

Again, shake the right hand and drop three coins onto the table. Tell the audience you will do it one last time.

STEP 7

Take one coin in your left hand and pretend to take it with your right. Use a transfer such as the French Drop. Pick up the rest of the coins with your left hand (there should be three in your left hand now) and put them in your pocket.

STEP 8

Ask the audience how many coins they think are in your right hand. Reveal that there are, in fact, no coins in your hands.

PRACTICE

all these tricks until you can amaze your friends and family. And remember, don't let them see this book. A true magician never reveals their secrets!

GLOSSARY

attention the notice taken of something

black magic evil magic

casually natural and normal looking

distract draw someone's attention away

knuckle the joints between the different parts of the finger

lap the area between the waist and knees when sitting down

palm the inside part of the hand between the wrist and fingers. Also, to hide something in this part of the hand.

performed put on a show for an audience

predict guess what is going to happen in the future

preparation practice put in beforehand

private not observed or disturbed by other people

prop an object used to help with a show

reappear appear again

reveal show or tell someone the answer to something secretive

tarot card a card used to read fortunes

teleport travel instantly

vague unclear

INDEX